1 MONTH OF
FREE
READING

at
www.ForgottenBooks.com

By purchasing this book you are eligible for one month membership to ForgottenBooks.com, giving you unlimited access to our entire collection of over 1,000,000 titles via our web site and mobile apps.

To claim your free month visit:
www.forgottenbooks.com/free795617

* Offer is valid for 45 days from date of purchase. Terms and conditions apply.

ISBN 978-0-483-70012-3
PIBN 10795617

This book is a reproduction of an important historical work. Forgotten Books uses state-of-the-art technology to digitally reconstruct the work, preserving the original format whilst repairing imperfections present in the aged copy. In rare cases, an imperfection in the original, such as a blemish or missing page, may be replicated in our edition. We do, however, repair the vast majority of imperfections successfully; any imperfections that remain are intentionally left to preserve the state of such historical works.

Forgotten Books is a registered trademark of FB &c Ltd.
Copyright © 2018 FB &c Ltd.
FB &c Ltd, Dalton House, 60 Windsor Avenue, London, SW19 2RR.
Company number 08720141. Registered in England and Wales.

For support please visit www.forgottenbooks.com

F291e1l

EGGLESTON, George C.

LIFE IN EARLY
INDIANA
(1910; rpt. 1953)

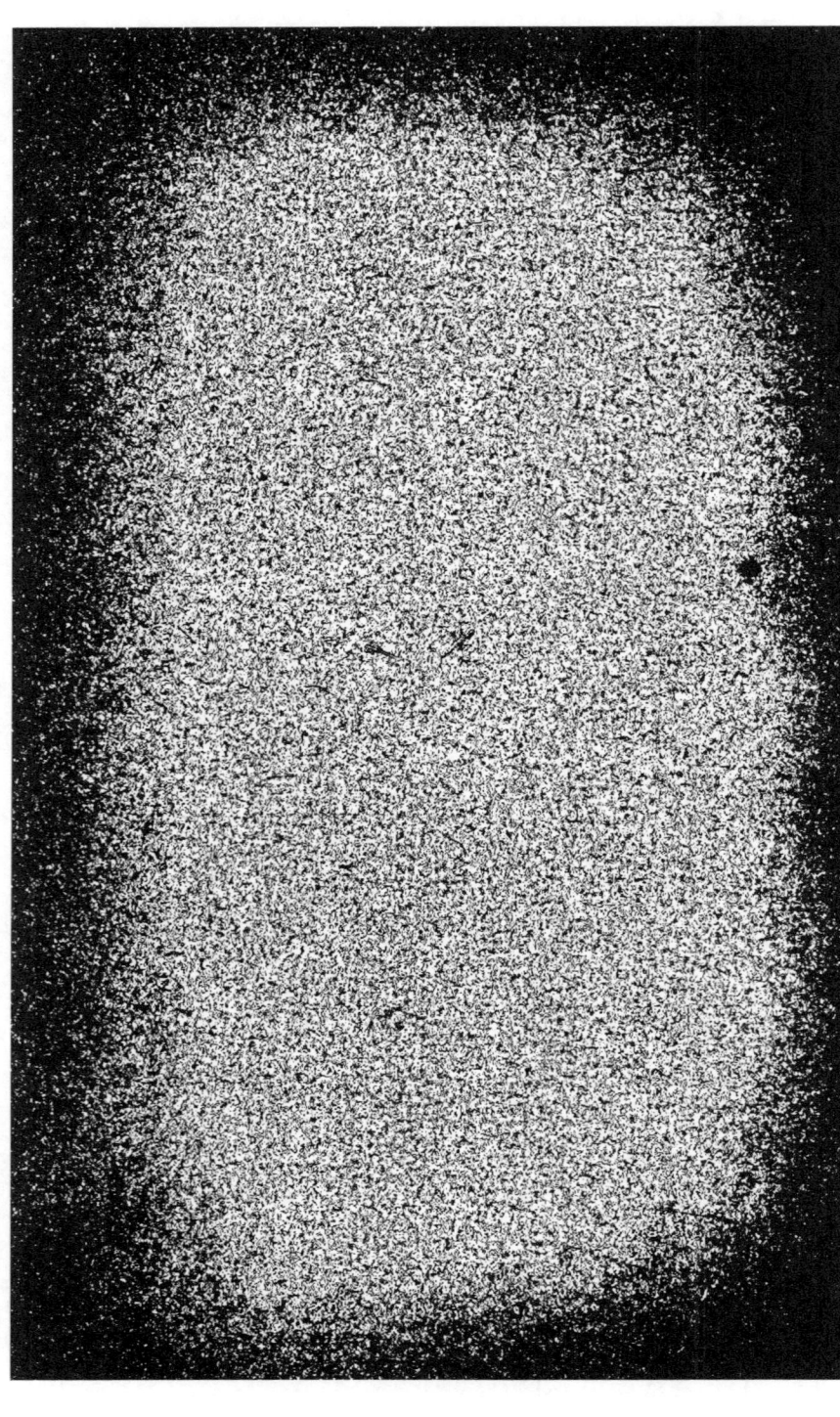

George Cary Eggleston

LIFE IN EARLY INDIANA

By George C. Eggleston

Prepared by the Staff of the
Public Library of Fort Wayne and Allen County
1953

One of a historical series, this pamphlet is published under the direction of the governing Boards of the Public Library of Fort Wayne and Allen County.

BOARD·OF·TRUSTEES·OF·THE·SCHOOL·CITY·OF·FORT·WAYNE

Mrs. Sadie Fulk Roehrs

W. Page Yarnelle, Treasurer

Joseph E. Kramer, Secretary

B.F. Geyer, President

Willard Shambaugh

PUBLIC LIBRARY BOARD FOR ALLEN COUNTY

The members of this Board include the members of the Board of Trustees of the School City of Fort Wayne (with the same officers) together with the following citizens chosen from Allen County outside the corporate City of Fort Wayne

James E. Graham

Arthur Niemeier

Mrs Glenn Henderson

Mrs. Charles Reynolds

FOREWORD

The coming of the railroads to the backwoods settlements of Indiana over a century ago was an event of major importance. The railroads speeded transportation and communication and brought waves of new settlers to the state. The economic and social life of the earlier pioneers was profoundly affected by the advent of the iron rails. Education, too, felt the impact of new ideas and new methods. In the following extract from RECOLLECTIONS OF A VARIED LIFE, these changes are vividly depicted.

George Cary Eggleston, author of the RECOLLECTIONS, was a native Hoosier. He was born in 1839 in the little town of Vevay. In later years, his newspaper work for the NEW YORK EVENING POST and the NEW YORK WORLD, his articles in the ATLANTIC MONTHLY and GALAXY magazines, and his series of books for boys brought him a measure of fame. His RECOLLECTIONS, published in 1910, is a leisurely autobiography enlivened by anecdotes of his early life and by characterizations of his newspaper and literary friends.

The following excerpt has been reprinted verbatim with the kind permission of the publishers, Henry Holt and Company. The Boards and the Staff of the Public Library of Fort Wayne and Allen County present the author's sketch of life in early Indiana in the hope that it will prove interesting to present-day Hoosiers.

THE life of that early time differed in every way from American life as men of the present day know it.

The isolation in which every community existed, compelled a degree of local self-dependence the like of which the modern world knows nothing of. The farmers did most things for themselves, and what they could not conveniently do for themselves, was done for them in the villages by independent craftsmen, each cunningly skilled in his trade and dependent upon factories for nothing. In my native village, Vevay, which was in nowise different from other Western villages upon which the region round about depended for supplies, practically everything wanted was made. There were two tinsmiths, who, with an assistant or two each, in the persons of boys learning the trade, made every utensil of tin, sheet-iron, or copper that was needed for twenty-odd miles around. There were two saddlers and harnessmakers; two or three plasterers; several brick masons; several carpenters, who knew their trade as no carpenter does in our time when the planing mill furnishes everything already shaped to his hand, so that the carpenter need know nothing but how to drive nails or screws. There was a boot- and shoemaker who made all the shoes worn by men, women, and children in all that country, out of leather bought of the local tanner, to whom all hides were sold by their producers. There was a hatter who did all his own work, whose vats yielded all the headgear needed, from the finest to the commonest, and whose materials were the furs of animals caught or killed by the farmers' boys and brought to town for sale. There was even a wireworker, who provided sieves, strainers, and screenings of every kind, and there was a rope walk where the cordage wanted was made.

In most households the women folk fashioned all the clothes worn by persons of either sex, but to meet the demand for "Sunday bests" and that of preachers who must wear broadcloth every day in the week, and of extravagant young men who wished to dazzle all eyes with "store clothes," there was a tailor who year after year fashioned garments upon models learned in his youth and never departed from. No such thing as ready-made clothing or boots or shoes—except women's slippers—was known at the time of which I now write. Even socks and stockings were never sold in the shops, except upon wedding and other infrequent occasions. For ordinary wear they were knitted at home of home-spun yarn. The statement made above is scarcely accurate. Both socks and stockings were occasionally sold in the country stores, but they were almost exclusively the surplus products of the industry of women on the farms round about. So were the saddle blankets, and most of the bed blankets used.

Local self-dependence was well-nigh perfect. The town depended on the country and the country on the town, for nearly everything that was eaten or woven or otherwise consumed. The day of dependence upon factories had not yet dawned. The man who knew how to fashion any article of human use, made his living by doing the work he knew how to do, and was an independent, self-respecting man, usually owning his comfortable home, and destined by middle age to possess a satisfactory competence.

Whether all that was economically or socially better than the system which has converted the independent, home-owning worker into a factory hand, living in a tenement and carrying a dinner pail, while tariff tribute from the consumer makes his employer at once a millionaire and the more or less despotic master of a multitude of men—is a question too large and too serious to be discussed in a book of random recollections such as this. But every " strike " raises that question in the minds of men who remember the more primitive conditions as lovingly as I do.

As a matter of curious historical interest, too, it is worth while to recall the fact that Henry Clay—before his desire to win the votes of the Kentucky hemp-growers led him to become the leading advocate of tariff protection—used to make eloquent speeches in behalf of free trade, in which he drew horrifying pictures of life conditions in the English manufacturing centers, and invoked the mercy of heaven to spare this country from like conditions in which economic considerations should ride down social ones, trample the life out of personal independence, and convert the home-owning American workman into a mere " hand " employed by a company of capitalists for their own enrichment at cost of his manhood except in so far as the fiat of a trades union might interpose to save him from slavery to the employing class.

Those were interesting speeches of Henry Clay's, made before he sacrificed his convictions and his manhood to his vain desire to become President.

II

At the time of my earliest recollections there was not a mile of railroad in Indiana or anywhere else west of Ohio, while even in Ohio there were only the crudest beginnings of track construction, on isolated lines that began nowhere and led no whither, connecting with nothing, and usually failing to make even that connection.

He who would journey from the East to the West, soon came to the end of the rails, and after that he must toilsomely make his way by stagecoach across the mountains, walking for the most part in mud half-leg deep, and carrying a fence rail on his shoulder with which to help the stalled stagecoach out of frequent mires.

Nevertheless, we heard much of the railroad and its wonders. It was our mystery story, our marvel, our current Arabian Nights' Entertainment. We were told, and devoutly believed, that the " railcars " ran at the rate of " a mile a minute." How or why the liars of that early period, when lying must have been in its infancy as an art, happened to hit upon sixty miles an hour as the uniform speed of railroad trains, I am puzzled to imagine. But so it was. There was probably not in all the world at that time a single mile of railroad track over which a train could have been run at such a speed. As for the railroads in the Western part of this country, they were chiefly primitive constructions, with tracks consisting of strap iron—wagon tires in effect—loosely spiked down to timber string pieces, over which it would have been reckless to the verge of insanity to run a train at more than twelve miles an hour under the most favorable circumstances. But we were told, over and over again, till we devoutly believed it—as human creatures always believe what they have been ceaselessly told without contradiction—that the " railcars " always ran at the rate of a mile a minute.

The first railroad in Indiana was opened in 1847. A year or two later, my brother Edward and I, made our first journey over it, from Madison to Dupont, a distance of thirteen miles. Edward was at that time a victim of the faith habit; I was beginning to manifest a skeptical, inquiring tendency of mind which distressed those responsible for me. When Edward reminded me that we were to enjoy our first experience of traveling at the rate of a mile a minute, I borrowed his bull's-eye watch and set myself to test the thing by timing it. When we reached Dupont, after the lapse of ninety-six minutes, in a journey of thirteen miles, I frankly declared my unbelief in the " mile a minute " tradition. There was no great harm in that, perhaps, but the skeptical spirit of inquiry that had prompted me to subject the matter to a time test, very seriously troubled my elders, who feared that I was destined to become a " free thinker," as my father had been before me, though I was not permitted to know that. I was alarmed about my skeptical tendencies myself, because I believed the theology and demonology taught me at church, having no means of subjecting them to scientific tests of any kind. I no longer believed in the "mile a minute " tradition, as everybody around me continued to do, but I still believed in the existence and malign activity of a personal devil, and I accepted the assurance given me that he was always at my side whispering doubts into my ears by way of securing the damnation of my soul under the doctrine of salvation by faith. The tortures I suffered on this account were well-nigh incredible, for in spite of all I might do or say or think, the doubts continued to arise in my mind, until at last I awoke to the fact that I was beginning to doubt the doctrine of salvation by faith itself, as a thing stultifying to the mind, unreasonable in itself, and utterly unjust in its application to persons like myself, who found it impossible to believe things which they had every reason to believe were not true.

Fortunately I was young and perfectly healthy, and so, after a deal of psychological suffering I found peace by

"..... and set myself to test the thing by timing it."....."

reconciling myself to the conviction that I was foreordained to be damned in any case, and that there was no use in making myself unhappy about it. In support of that comforting assurance I secretly decided to accept the Presbyterian doctrine of predestination instead of the Methodist theory of free will in which I had been bred. I had to make this change of doctrinal allegiance secretly, because its open avowal would have involved a sound threshing behind the smoke-house, with perhaps a season of fasting and prayer, designed to make the castigation "take."

I remember that when I had finally made up my mind that the doctrine of predestination was true, and that I was clearly one of those who were foreordained to be damned for incapacity to believe the incredible, I became for a time thoroughly comfortable in my mind, very much as I suppose a man of business is when he receives his discharge in bankruptcy. I felt myself emancipated from many restraints that had sat heavily on my boyish soul. Having decided, with the mature wisdom of ten or a dozen years of age, that I was to be damned in any case, I saw no reason why I should not read the fascinating books that had been forbidden to me by the discipline of the Methodist Church, to which I perforce belonged.

In that early day of strenuous theological requirement, the Methodist Church disapproved of literature as such, and approved it only in so far as it was made the instrument of a propaganda. Its discipline required that each person upon being "received into full membership"—the Methodist equivalent of confirmation—should take a vow not "to read such books or sing such songs as do not pertain to the glory of God." I quote the phrase from memory, but accurately I think. That prohibition, as interpreted by clerical authority at the time, had completely closed to me the treasures of the library my scholarly father had collected, and to which, under his dying instructions, my mother had added many scores of volumes of the finest English literature, purchased with the money for which his law books had been sold after his death.

I had read a little here and there in those books, and had been fascinated with the new world they opened to my vision, when, at the ripe age of ten or twelve years, I was compelled by an ill-directed clerical authority to submit myself to the process of being "received into full membership," under the assumption that I had "reached the age of responsibility."

After that the books I so longed to read were forbidden to me—especially a set entitled "The British Drama," in which appeared the works of Ben Jonson, Marlowe, Massinger, Beaumont and Fletcher, and a long list of other classics, filling five thick volumes. By no ingenuity of construction could such books be regarded as homilies in disguise, and so they were Anathema. So was Shakespeare, and so even was Thiers' "French Revolution," of which I had devoured the first volume in delight, before the inhibition fell upon me, blasting my blind but eager aspiration for culture and a larger knowledge of the world and of human nature.

III

AFTER I made up my mind to accept damnation as my appointed portion, I felt myself entirely free to revel at will in the reading that so appealed to my hungry mind; free, that is to say, so far as my own conscience was concerned, but no freer than before so far as the restraints of authority could determine the matter. I had no hesitation in reading the books when I could do so without being caught at it, but to be caught at it was to be punished for it and, worse still, it was to have the books placed beyond my reach, a thing I dreaded far more than mere punishment. Punishment, indeed, seemed to me nothing more than a small advance upon the damnation I must ultimately suffer in any case. The thing to be avoided was discovery, because discovery must lead to the confiscation of my books, the loss of that liberty which my acceptance of damnation had given to me.

To that end I practised many deceits and resorted to many subterfuges. I read late at night when I was supposed to be asleep. I smuggled books out into the woods and hid them there under the friendly roots of trees, so that I might go out and read them when I was supposed to be engaged in a search for ginseng, or in a hunt for the vagrant cow, to whose unpunctuality in returning to be milked I feel that I owe an appreciable part of such culture as I have acquired.

The clerical hostility to literature endured long after the period of which I have been writing, long after the railroad and other means of freer intercourse had redeemed the West from its narrow provincialism. Even in my high school days, when our part of the country had reached that stage of civilization that hangs lace curtains at its windows, wears store clothes of week days, and paints garden fences green instead of white, we who were under Methodist dominance were rigidly forbidden to read fiction or anything that resembled fiction, with certain exceptions. The grown folk of our creed permitted themselves to read the inane novels of the Philadelphia tailor, T. S. Arthur; the few young men who "went to college," were presumed to be immune to the virus of the Greek and Latin fictions they must read there—probably because they never learned enough of Greek or Latin to read them understandingly—and finally there were certain polemic novels that were generally permitted.

Among these last the most conspicuous example I re-

"... I read late at night ..."

member was a violently anti-Roman Catholic novel called "Danger in the Dark," which had a vogue that the "best-sellers" of our later time might envy. It was not only permitted to us to read that—it was regarded as our religious duty in order that we might learn to hate the Catholics with increased fervor.

The religious animosities of that period, with their relentless intolerance, their unreason, their matchless malevolence, and their eagerness to believe evil, ought to form an interesting and instructive chapter in some history of civilization in America, whenever a scholar of adequate learning and the gift of interpretation shall undertake that work. But that is a task for some Buckle or Lecky. It does not belong to a volume of random reminiscences such as this is.

IV

THOUGH the railroads, when at last they came to us, failed utterly in their promise of transportation at the rate of "a mile a minute," they did something else, presently, that was quite as remarkable and far worthier in its way. They ran down and ran over, and crushed out of existence a provincialism that had much of evil promise and very little of present good in it. With their coming, and in some degree in advance of their coming, a great wave of population poured into the West from all quarters of the country. The newcomers brought with them their ideas, their points of view, their convictions, their customs, and their standards of living. Mingling together in the most intimate ways, socially and in business pursuits, each lost something of his prejudices and provincialism, and gained much by contact with men of other ways of thinking and living. Attrition sharpened the perceptions of all and smoothed away angles of offense. A spirit of tolerance was awakened such as had never been known in the Western country before, and as the West became populous and prosperous, it became also more broadly and generously American, more truly national in character, and more accurately representative of all that is best in American thought and life than any part of the country had ever been. It represented the whole country and all its parts.

The New Englanders, the Virginians, the Pennsylvanians, the Carolinians, the Kentuckians, who were thus brought together into composite communities with now and then an Irish, a French, a Dutch, or a German family, a group of Switzers, and a good many Scotchmen for neighbors and friends, learned much and quickly each from all the others. Better still, each unlearned the prejudices, the bigotries, and the narrownesses in which he had been bred, and life in the great West took on a liberality of mind, a breadth of tolerance and sympathy, a generous humanity such as had never been known in any of the narrowly provincial regions that furnished the materials of this composite population. It seems to me scarcely too much to say that real Americanism, in the broad sense of the term, had its birth in that new "winning of the West," which the railroads achieved about the middle of the nineteenth century.

With the coming of easier and quicker communication, not only was the West brought into closer relations with the East, but the West itself became quickly more homogeneous. There was a constant shifting of population from one place to another, much traveling about, and a free interchange of thought among a people who were eagerly alert to adopt new ideas that seemed in any way to be better than the old. As I recall the rapid changes of that time it seems to me that the betterments came with a rapidity rarely if ever equaled in human history. A year or two at that time was sufficient to work a revolution even in the most conservative centers of activity. Changes of the most radical kind and involving the most vital affairs, were made over-night, as it were, and with so little shock to men's minds that they ceased, almost immediately, to be topics of conversation. The old had scarcely passed away before it was forgotten, and the new as quickly became the usual, the ordinary, the familiar order of things.

V

I DO not mean to suggest that the West, or indeed any other part of the country, at once put aside all its crudities of custom and adopted the ways of living that we are familiar with in this later time. All that has been a thing of gradual accomplishment, far slower in its coming than most people realize.

I remember that when Indianapolis became a great railroad center and a city of enormous proportions—population from 15,000 to 20,000, according to the creative capacity of the imagination making the estimate—a wonderful hotel was built there, and called the Bates House. Its splendors were the subject of wondering comment throughout the West. It had washstands, with decorated pottery on them, in all its more expensive rooms, so that a guest sojourning there need not go down to the common washroom for his morning ablution, and dry his hands and face on a jack-towel. There were combs and brushes in the rooms, too, so that if one wanted to smooth his hair he was not obliged to resort to the appliances of that sort that were hung by chains to the washroom walls.

Moreover, if a man going to the Bates House for a sojourn, chose to pay a trifle extra he might have a room all to himself, without the prospect of being waked up in the middle of the night to admit some stranger, assigned by the hotel authorities to share his room and bed.

All these things were marvels of pretentious luxury, borrowed from the more " advanced " hostelries of the Eastern cities, and as such they became topics of admiring comment everywhere, as illustrations of the wonderful progress of civilization that was taking place among us.

But all these subjects of wonderment shrank to nothingness by comparison, when the proprietors of the Bates House printed on their breakfast bills of fare, an announcement that thereafter each guest's breakfast would be cooked after his order for it was given, together with an appeal for patience on the part of the breakfasters—a patience that the proprietors promised to reward with hot and freshly prepared dishes.

This innovation was so radical that it excited discussion hotter even than the Bates House breakfasts. Opinions differed as to the right of a hotel keeper to make his guests wait for the cooking of their breakfasts. To some minds the thing presented itself as an invasion of personal liberty and therefore of the constitutional rights of the citizen. To others it seemed an intolerable nuisance, while by those who were ambitious of reputation as persons who had traveled and were familiar with good usage, it was held to be a welcome advance in civilization. In approving it, they were able to exploit themselves as persons who had not only traveled as far as the state capital, but while there had paid the two dollars a day, which the Bates House charged for entertainment, instead of going to less pretentious taverns where the customary charge of a dollar or a dollar and a half a day still prevailed, and where breakfast was put upon the table before

"...waked up in the middle of the night..."

the gong invited guests to rush into the dining room and madly scramble for what they could get of it.

In the same way I remember how we all wondered over the manifestation of luxury made by the owners of a newly built steamboat of the Louisville and Cincinnati Mail Line, when we heard that the several staterooms were provided with wash-basins. That was in the fifties. Before that time, two common washrooms—one for men and the other for women—had served all the passengers on each steamboat, and, as those washrooms had set-bowls with running water, they were regarded as marvels of sumptuousness in travel facilities. It was partly because of such luxury, I suppose, that we called the steamboats of that time "floating palaces." They seemed so then. They would not impress us in that way now. Perhaps fifty years hence the great ocean liners of the present, over whose perfection of equipment we are accustomed to wonder, will seem equally unworthy. Such things are comparative and the world moves fast.

VI

THE crudities here referred to, however, are not properly to be reckoned as belonging exclusively to the West, or as specially indicative of the provincialism of the West. At that time and for long afterward, it was usual, even in good hotels throughout the country, to assign two men, wholly unacquainted with each other, to occupy a room in common. It was expected that the hotel would provide a comb and brush for the use of guests in each room, as the practice of carrying one's own toilet appliances of that kind had not yet become general. Hotel rooms with private bathrooms adjoining, were wholly unknown before the Civil War, and the practice of taking a daily bath was very uncommon indeed. A hotel guest asking for such a thing would have been pointed out to bystanders as a curiosity of effete dandyism. Parenthetically, I may say that as late as 1886 I engaged for my wife and myself a room with private bath on the first floor of the Nadeau House, then the best hotel in Los Angeles, California. The man at the desk explained that the bathroom did not open directly into the room, but adjoined it and was accessible from the dead end of the hallway without. We got on very well with this arrangement until Saturday night came, when, as I estimated the number, all the unmarried men of the city took turns in bathing in my private bathroom. When I entered complaint at the desk next morning, the clerk evidently regarded me as a monster of arrogant selfishness. He explained that as I had free use of the bathroom every day and night of the week, I ought not to feel aggrieved at its invasion by other cleanly disposed persons on " the usual night for taking a bath."

The experience brought two facts to my attention: first, that in the opinion of the great majority of my fellow American citizens one bath a week was quite sufficient, and, second, that the fixed bathtub, with hot and cold water running directly into it, is a thing of comparatively modern use. I suppose that in the eighteen-fifties, and quite certainly in the first half of that decade, there were no such appliances of luxurious living in any but the very wealthiest houses, if even there. Persons who wanted an " all-over bath," went to a barber shop for it, if they lived in a city, and, if they lived elsewhere, went without it, or pressed a family washtub into friendly service.

So, too, as late as 1870, in looking for a house in Brooklyn, I found it difficult to get one of moderate rent cost, that had other water supply than such as a hydrant in the back yard afforded.

".. all the unmarried men of the city took turns in bathing .."

VII

To return to the changes wrought in the West by the construction of railroads and the influx of immigration from all parts of the country. In nothing else was the improvement more rapid or more pronounced than in education. Until the early fifties, and even well into them, educational endeavors and educational methods were crude, unorganized, wasteful of effort, and utterly uncertain of result. From the very beginning the desire for education had been alert and eager in the West, and the readiness to spend money and effort in that behalf had been unstinted. But the means were lacking and system was lacking. More important still there was lack of any well-considered or fairly uniform conception of what education ought to aim at or achieve.

In the rural districts schools were sporadic and uncertain. When a "master" was available "school kept," and its chief activity was to teach the spelling of the English language. Incidentally it taught pupils to read and the more advanced ones—ten per cent. of all, perhaps, to write. As a matter of higher education rudimentary arithmetic had a place in the curriculum. Now and then a schoolmaster appeared who essayed other things in a desultory way but without results of any consequence. In the villages and towns the schools were usually better, but even there the lack of any well-ordered system was a blight.

The schoolmasters were frequently changed, for one thing, each newcoming one bringing his own notions to bear upon problems that he was not destined to remain long enough to solve. Even in the more permanent schools, kept by very young or superannuated preachers, or by Irish schoolmasters who conducted them on the "knock down and drag out" system, there was no attempt to frame a scheme of education that should aim at well conceived results. In every such school there were two or three boys taking "the classical course," by which was meant that without the least question or consideration of their fitness to do so, they had dropped all ordinary school studies and were slowly plodding along in rudimentary Latin, in obedience to some inherited belief on the part of their parents that education consists in studying Latin, that there is a benediction in a paradigm, and that fitness for life's struggle is most certainly achieved by the reading of "Historia Sacra," "Cornelius Nepos," and the early chapters of "Cæsar's Commentaries on the Gallic War."

Other pupils, under the impression that they were taking a "scientific course," were drilled in Comstock's Physiology and Natural Philosophy, and somebody's "Geography of the Heavens." The rest of the school—plebeians all—contented themselves with reading, writing, arithmetic, geography, and a vain attempt to master the mysteries and mists of Kirkham's Grammar.

The railroads quickly changed all this. They brought into the West men and women who knew who Horace Mann was, and whose conceptions of education in its aims and methods were definite, well ordered, and aggressive.

These set to work to organize graded school systems in the larger towns, and the thing was contagious, in a region where every little town was confidently ambitious of presently becoming the most important city in the state, and did not intend in the meantime to permit any other to outdo it in the frills and furbelows of largeness.

With preparatory education thus organized and systematized, and with easy communication daily becoming easier, the ambition of young men to attend colleges and universities was more and more gratified, so that within a very few years the higher education—so far as it is represented by college courses—became common throughout the country, while for those who could not achieve that, or were not minded to do so, the teaching of the schools was adapted, as it never had been before, to the purpose of real, even if meager education.

Even in the remotest country districts a new impetus was given to education, and the subjection of the schools there to the supervision of school boards and professional superintendents worked wonders of reformation. For one thing the school boards required those who wished to serve as teachers to pass rigid examinations in test of their fitness, so that it was no longer the privilege of any ignoramus who happened to be out of a job to "keep school." In addition to this the school boards prescribed and regulated the courses of study, the classification of pupils, and the choice of text-books, even in country districts where graded schools were not to be thought of, and this supervision gave a new and larger meaning to school training in the country.

VIII

It was my fortune to be the first certified teacher under this system in a certain rural district where the old haphazard system had before prevailed, and my experience there connects itself interestingly, I think, with a bit of literary history. It was the instigation of my brother, Edward Eggleston's, most widely popular story, "The Hoosier Schoolmaster," which in its turn was the instigation of all the fascinating literature that has followed it with Hoosier life conditions for its theme.

My school district lay not many miles from the little town in which my family lived, and as I had a good pair of legs, well used to walking, I went home every Friday night, returning on Monday morning after a four o'clock breakfast. On these week-end visits it was my delight to tell of the queer experiences of the week, and Edward's delight to listen to them while he fought against the maladies that were then threatening his brave young life with early extinction.

Years afterwards he and I were together engaged in an effort to resuscitate the weekly illustrated newspaper *Hearth and Home,* which had calamitously failed to win a place for itself, under a number of highly distinguished editors, whose abilities seemed to compass almost everything except the art of making a newspaper that people wanted and would pay for. Of that effort I shall perhaps have more to say in a future chapter. It is enough now to say that the periodical had a weekly stagnation— it will not do to call it a circulation—of only five or six thousand copies, nearly half of them gratuitous, and it had netted an aggregate loss of many thousands of dollars to the several publishers who had successively made themselves its sponsors. It was our task—Edward's and mine—to make the thing "pay," and to that end both of us were cudgeling our brains by day and by night to devise means.

One evening a happy thought came to Edward and he hurriedly quitted whatever he was doing to come to my house and submit it.

"I have a mind, Geordie," he said, "to write a three number story, called 'The Hoosier Schoolmaster,' and to found it upon your experience at Riker's Ridge."

We talked the matter over. He wrote and published the first of the three numbers, and its popularity was instant. The publishers pleaded with him, and so did

I, to abandon the three number limitation, and he yielded. Before the serial publication of the story ended, the subscription list of *Hearth and Home* had been many times multiplied and Edward Eggleston was famous.

He was far too original a man, and one possessed of an imagination too fertilely creative to follow at all closely my experiences, which had first suggested the story to him. He made one or two personages among my pupils the models from which he drew certain of his characters, but beyond that the experiences which suggested the story in no way entered into its construction. Yet in view of the facts it seems to me worth while to relate something of those suggestive experiences.

I was sixteen years old when I took the school. Circumstances had compelled me for the time to quit college, where, despite my youthfulness, I was in my second year. The Riker's Ridge district had just been brought under supervision of the school authorities at Madison. A new schoolhouse had been built and a teacher was wanted to inaugurate the new system. I applied for the place, stood the examinations, secured my certificate, and was appointed.

On my first appearance in the neighborhood, the elders there seemed distinctly disappointed in the selection made. They knew the school history of the district. They remembered that the last three masters had been " licked " by stalwart and unruly boys, the last one so badly that he had abandoned the school in the middle of the term. They strongly felt the need, therefore, of a master of mature years, strong arms, and ponderous fists as the person chosen to inaugurate the new system. When a beardless boy of sixteen presented himself instead, they shook their heads in apprehension. But the appointment had been made by higher authority, and they had no choice but to accept it. Appreciating the nature of their fears,

"....my first appearance.."

I told the grave and reverend seigniors that my schoolboy experience had shown my arms to be stronger, my fists heavier, and my nimbleness greater perhaps than they imagined, but that in the conduct of the school I should depend far more upon the diplomatic nimbleness of my wits than upon physical prowess, and that I thought I should manage to get on.

There was silence for a time. Then one wise old patriarch said:

"Well, may be so. But there's Charley Grebe. You wouldn't make a mouthful for him. Anyhow, we'll see, we'll see."

Charley Grebe was the youth who had thrashed the last master so disastrously.

Thus encouraged, I went to my task.

The neighborhood was in no sense a bad one. There were none of the elements in it that gave character to "Flat Creek" as depicted in "The Hoosier Schoolmaster." The people were all quiet, orderly, entirely reputable folk, most of them devotedly pious. They were mainly of "Pennsylvania Dutch" extraction, stolid on the surface but singularly emotional within. But the school traditions of the region were those of the old time, when the master was regarded as the common enemy, who must be thwarted in every possible way, resisted at every point where resistance was possible, and "thrashed" by the biggest boy in school if the biggest boy could manage that.

There was really some justification for this attitude of the young Americans in every such district. For under the old system, as I very well remember it, the government of schools was brutal, cruel, inhuman in a degree that might in many cases have excused if it did not justify a homicidal impulse on the part of its victims. The boys of the early time would never have grown into the stalwart Americans who fought the Civil War if they had submitted to such injustice and so cruel a tyranny without making the utmost resistance they could.

IX

I BEGAN my work with a little friendly address to the forty or fifty boys and girls who presented themselves as pupils. I explained to them that my idea of a school was quite different from that which had before that time prevailed in that region; that I was employed by the authorities to teach them all I could, by way of fitting them for life, and that I was anxious to do that in the case of every boy and girl present. I expressed the hope that they in their turn were anxious to learn all I could teach them, and that if any of them found their studies too difficult, I would gladly give my time out of school hours to the task of discovering the cause of the difficulty and remedying it. I explained that in my view government in a school should have no object beyond that of giving every pupil opportunity to learn all he could, and the teacher opportunity to teach all he could. I frankly abolished the arbitrary rule that had before made of whispering a grave moral offense, and substituted for it a request that every pupil should be careful not to disturb the work of others in any way, so that we might all make the most of our time and opportunity.

It was a new gospel, and in the main it fell upon deaf ears. A few of the pupils were impressed by its reasonableness and disposed to meet the new teacher half way. The opinion of the majority was expressed by one boy whom I overheard at recess when he said to one of his fellows:

"He's skeered o' Charley Grebe, an' he's a-tryin' to soft-sawder us."

The first day or two of school were given to the rather perplexing work of classifying pupils whose previous instruction had been completely at haphazard. During that process I minutely observed the one foe against whom I had received more than one warning—Charley Grebe. He was a young man of nearly twenty-one, six feet, one or two inches high, broad-shouldered, muscular, and with a jaw that suggested all the relentless determination that one young man can hold.

When I questioned him with a view to his classification, he was polite enough in his uninstructed way, but exceedingly reserved. On the whole he impressed me as a young man of good natural ability, who had been discouraged by bad and incapable instruction. After he had told me, rather grudgingly I thought, what ground his studies had covered, he suddenly changed places with me and became the questioner.

"Say," he broke out, interrupting some formal question of mine, "Say, do you know anything in fact? Do you know Arithmetic an' Algebra an' Geometry and can you really teach me? or are you just pretending, like the rest?"

I thought I understood him and I guessed what his experience had been. I assured him that there was nothing in Arithmetic that I could not teach him, that I knew my Algebra, Geometry, and Trigonometry, and could help him to learn them, if he really desired to do so. Then adopting something of his own manner I asked:

"What is it you want me to do, Charley? Say what you have to say, like a man, and don't go beating about the bush."

For reply, he said:

"I want to talk with you. It'll be a long talk. I

"He's skeered o' Charley Grebe.."

want you to go home with me to-night. Father said I might invite you. Will you come?"

There was eager earnestness in his questions, but there was also a note of discouragement, if not quite of despair in his tone. I agreed at once to go with him for the night, and, taking the hand he had not thought of offering, I added:

"If there is any way in which I can help you, Charley, I'll do it gladly."

Whether it was the unaccustomed courtesy, or the awakening of a new hope, or something else, I know not, but the awkward, overgrown boy seemed at once to assume the dignity of manhood, and while he had never been taught to say "thank you" or to use any other conventionally polite form of speech, he managed to make me understand by his manner that he appreciated my offer, and a few minutes later, school having been dismissed, he and I set out for his home.

There he explained his case to me. He wanted to become a shipwright—a trade which, in that time of multitudinous steamboat building on the Western rivers, was the most inviting occupation open to a young man of energy. He had discovered that a man who wished to rise to anything like a mastery in that trade must have a good working knowledge of Arithmetic, elementary Algebra, Geometry, and at least the rudiments of Trigonometry. He had wanted to learn these things and some of his previous schoolmasters had undertaken to teach them, with no result except presently to reveal to him their own ignorance. His father permitted him six months more of schooling. He had "sized me up," he said, and he believed I could teach him what he wanted to learn. But could he learn it within six months? That was what he wanted me to tell him. I put him through a close examination in Arithmetic that night—consuming most of the night—and before morning I had satisfied myself that he was an apt pupil who, with diligence and such earnest determination as he manifested, could learn what he really needed of mathematics within the time named.

"You can do it, Charley, if you work hard, and I'll help you, in school hours and out," was my final verdict.

"It's a bargain," he said, and that was all he said. But a day or two later a boy in school—a great, hulking fellow whose ugliness of disposition I had early discerned—made a nerve-racking noise by dragging his pencil over his slate in a way that disturbed the whole school. I bade him cease, but he presently repeated the offense. Again I rebuked him, but five minutes or so later he defiantly did the thing again, "just to see if the master dared," he afterward explained. Thereupon Charley Grebe arose, seized the fellow by the ear, twisted that member until its owner howled with pain, and then, hurling him back into his seat, said:

"*You heard the master! You'll mind him after this or I'll make you.*"

The event fairly appalled the school. The thought that Charley Grebe was on the master's side, and actively helping him to maintain discipline, seemed beyond belief. But events soon confirmed it. There was a little fellow in the school whom everybody loved, and whose quaint, childish ways afterwards suggested the character of "Shocky" in "The Hoosier Schoolmaster." There was also a cowardly brute there whose delight it was to persecute the little fellow on the playground in intolerable ways. I sought to stop the thing. To that end I devised and inflicted every punishment I could think of, short of flogging, but all to no purpose. At last I laid aside my convictions with my patience, and gave the big bully such a flogging as must have impressed his mind if he had had anything of the kind about his person.

"You heard the master!"

That day, at the noon recess, the big bully set to work to beat the little boy unmercifully in revenge for what I had done for his protection. I was looking out through a Venetian blind, with intent to go to the rescue, when suddenly Charley Grebe, who was playing town ball threw down the bat, seized the fellow, threw him across his knees, pinioned his legs with one of his own, and literally wore out a dozen or more thick blue ash shingles over that part of his victim's body which was made for spanking.

When at last he released the blubbering object of his wrath he slapped his jaws soundly and said:

"Don't you go a-whining to the master about this. If you do it'll be a good deal wuss for you. I'm a-takin' this here job off the master's hands."

I gave no hint that I had seen or heard. But from that hour forth no boy in the school ever gave me the smallest trouble by misbehavior. The school perfectly understood that Charley Grebe was "a-takin' this here job off the master's hands," and the knowledge was sufficient.

After that only the big girls—most of them older than I was—gave me trouble. I met it with the explanation that I could never think of punishing a young woman, and that I must trust to their honor and courtesy, as girls who expected presently to be ladies, for their behavior. The appeal was a trifle slow in eliciting a response, but in the end it answered its purpose.

X

WHILE I was enrolling and classifying the pupils, I encountered a peculiarly puzzling case. There were five John Riddels in the school, and I found that all of them were sons of the same man, whose name also was John Riddel. No one of them had a middle name or any other sort of name by which he might be distinguished from his brothers. On the playground they were severally known as "Big John Riddel," "John Riddel," "Johnny Riddel," "Little John Riddel," and "Little Johnny Riddel," while their father was everywhere known as "Old John Riddel," though he was a man under fifty, I should say. He lived near, in a stone house, with stone barns and out-houses, an ingeniously devised milk-house, and a still more ingeniously constructed device for bringing water from the spring under the hill into his dwelling.

In brief his thrift was altogether admirable, and the mechanical devices by which he made the most of every opportunity, suggested a fertilely inventive mind on the part of a man whose general demeanor was stolid to the verge of stupidity. When I was taking supper at his house one night by special invitation, I asked him why he had named all his sons John. For reply he said:

"John is a very good name," and that was all the explanation I ever got out of him.

XI

ONE pupil I had at Riker's Ridge, was Johnny G. His people had some money and Johnny had always dressed better than the rest of us could afford to do, when several years before, he and I had been classmates in the second or third grade of the Grammar School in Madison, Johnny had never got out of that grade, and even when I was in my second year in college, he gave no promise of ever making a scholastic step forward. But he had relatives on Riker's Ridge, and when he heard that I was to be the teacher there he promised his people that he would really make an effort if they would let him live with his relatives there and become my pupil. It was so arranged, and Johnny came to me, with all his dazzling waistcoats and trousers with the latest style of pockets, and all the rest of the upholstery with which he delighted to decorate his person.

I think he really did make an effort to master the rudimentary school studies, and I conscientiously endeavored to help him, not only in school but of evenings. For a time there seemed to be a reasonable promise of success in lifting Johnny to that level of scholastic attainment which would permit him to return to Madison and enter the High School. But presently all this was brought to naught. Johnny was seized by a literary ambition that completely absorbed what mind he had, and made his school studies seem to him impertinent intrusions upon the attention of one absorbed in higher things.

He told me all about it one afternoon as I walked homeward with him, intent upon finding out why he had suddenly ceased to get his lessons.

"I'm going to write a song," he told me, "and it's going to make me famous. I'm writing it now, and I tell you it's fine."

"Tell me about it, Johnny," I replied. "What is its theme? And how much of it have you written?"

"I don't know what it's to be about," he answered, "if that's what you mean by its theme. But it's going to be great, and I'm going to make the tune to it myself."

"Very well," I replied encouragingly. "Would you mind reciting to me so much of it as you've written? I'd like to hear it."

"Why, of course. I tell you it's going to be great, but I haven't got much of it done yet—only one line, in fact."

"I'm going to write a song."

Observing a certain discouragement in his tone I responded:

"Oh, well, even one line is a good deal, if it's good. Many a poem's fortune has been made by a single line. Tell me what it is."

"Well, the line runs: 'With a pitcher of buttermilk under her arm.' Don't you see how it sort o' sings? 'With a pitcher of buttermilk under her arm'—why, it's great, I tell you. Confound the school books! What's the use of drudging when a fellow has got it in him to write poetry like that? 'With a pit-cher of but-termilk un-der her arm'—don't it sing? 'With a *pit*-cher of but-termilk un-der her arm.' 'With a *pit*-cher of *but*-termilk—un-der her arm.' Whoopee, but it's great!"

I lost sight of Johnny soon after that, and I have never heard what became of that buttermilk pitcher, or the fascinating rhythm in which it presented itself. But in later years I have come into contact with many literary ambitions that were scarcely better based than this. Indeed, if I were minded to be cynical—as I am not—I might mention a few magazine poets whose pitchers of buttermilk seem to me—but all that is foreign to the purpose of this book.

Before quitting this chapter and the period and region to which it relates, I wish to record that Charley Grebe mastered the mathematics he needed, and entered hopefully upon his apprenticeship to a ship carpenter. I hope he rose to the top in the trade, but I know nothing about it.